JENNIE WADE:
A GIRL FROM
GETTYSBURG

By Tecla Emerson

Cover Design by
Katharine Sodergreen
Sodergreen@aol.com

Formatting by
Robert Louis Henry
http://leafgardenpress.com

ISBN-13:978-1491090244
ISBN-10:1491090243

Dedicated to my three favorite young readers:
Adeline, Juliet and Katie

TABLE OF CONTENTS

"And in the end it is not the years in your life that count, it's the life in your years."

~ Abraham Lincoln

~ PROLOGUE ~

This is the story of Ginnie, or Jennie, as they called her later in that newspaper article. Name stuck from that day on. The only people who even remembered she was supposed to be Ginnie was Mother, John James and Samuel, and, of course, my Louis. But then they wanted to mess up his name too by spelling it Lewis. Harry, the youngest in our family, didn't know the difference. But if truth be known, he was the one who said, "If her real name was Mary Virginia Wade, where'd they get Jennie from?"

But that's where it all started. Everyone pretty much got to know her name, after that battle and all. What with only one civilian killed that day, it wasn't too hard to remember what her name was. They always got mine right, or at least the shortened one that my family always called me. Georgie isn't too awfully difficult.

Jennie, as I now call her so's people will know who it is I'm talking about, was my sister. I called her my baby sister when we were growing up in southern Pennsylvania, up 'til the Civil War anyhow. At 13, she grew some and got to be just a mite taller than me. Maybe it was a bit more than a mite. Anyways, after that my brothers always got a chuckle out of me referring to her as my little sister. That was the year that she suddenly got pretty, too. Up to that point she'd been gangly, mostly arms and legs, and a bit awkward, almost like a scarecrow that'd come to life. Mother said to leave her be, she'd be a fine young lady soon enough.

Seemed like almost overnight she went from that skinny freckle-faced little tomboy, who got into a fair amount of trouble, into an almost graceful young lady. I think maybe it had to do with Johnston Skelly, who by the way, went by the name Jack! Don't know where that came from either. So, he hadn't actually come calling yet, Jack that is, but I'd seen him a few times down on the corner, down by Miller's Feed Store. He'd be just kind of hanging around, whittling at some piece of wood, making like he was busy and wait for her to pass by. Kinda funny when you would see them greet each other with nods, like they were strangers.

They'd been great playmates in grade school, but something seemed to happen when she started putting her braids up 'stead of letting them hang loose down her back. Everything changed then. All of a sudden they'd gotten shy with each other. They used to just outright laugh and play and chase each other all over everywhere, having a gay old time. Now all of a sudden, Jennie would just up and blush when he came near.

Those two used to sled together up on the hill just north of town and have more fun. Then they'd chase each other and play tag and get everyone involved in hide-and-seek. They were more like two rambunctious brothers, always getting into some kind of mischief. Well, as I said, things sure did change in a heartbeat.

For two sisters though, we were pretty good friends, Jennie and I, at least for the last couple of years. We'd rubbed each other wrong growing up sometimes. You can imagine, what with us being just a year and 10 months apart.

Mother favored her, I always knew that. I mean she was the prettiest and all. I was the smartest they said, but that sure didn't count for much when school let out. We used to fight somethin' terrible, I'll tell you. Mother had to come and break up more than one tangle that we'd gotten into. And it was always me who got into the worst danged trouble. 'Scuse me. No need for me to be cursing. But, I was older; I was supposed to know better and so I was the one who caught it.

Once, I remember that Jennie made me so mad I tried to pull her braids off her head. Ha! Makes me laugh now to remember. Well I probably would've got it done except that was when Samuel ran and got Father's old Springfield rifle off the wall. He said he'd shoot us both if we didn't quit. Well it wasn't so much the fear of being shot by little Samuel as it was the sight of him, all of about five years old, dragging that old Springfield into the room with it clanging along behind him, thinking he was actually going to use it. We all three ended up in a heap on the floor laughing 'til our sides about split.

Jennie had my favorite hair ribbons on that day. Never forgot it either. They were mine. My father gave them to me special just before Mother sent him away. And there was Jennie, flouncing around with my ribbons in her tangled mass of curls. Imagine!

Most often her hair was a mess, especially when she didn't take the time to comb through it or do her braids. It was a chestnut color, usually all shiny. If she plaited it in the morning it would stay neat and tidy for just a while, and then curls would start to escape as the day wore on. It kind of framed her face, all those nice soft curls. Most girls use a curling iron to get their hair to look like that; anyways that's how they do it around here. I hated that head of hair. It was always pretty and curly and it was forever escaping from under her mop cap or coming undone at the most inopportune moments; then there'd be this cascade of bouncing curls trailing down her back. Mine was as straight as hair can get. Mother said Jennie had father's hair, wiry and unruly, and said she was just going to have to live with it. She of course found it too much trouble to be messin' with, which is why it was always flying off in all directions.

Wasn't fair I told them. I was older but Jennie was taller and prettier. She had these really deep brown eyes that just sort of bored into you when she looked at you and she had this way of acting like you were the only person in the room when you spoke to her. I mean she'd just turn her entire attention on you like whatever you had to say was the most important thing she'd ever heard. Those eyes. Came from the German side, Mother said. Most times they were laughing, always crinkling up at the corners and looking around for what's next. Everyone loved her. She had no enemies that I ever heard tell of. Don't know how she did it, but she did.

She was a busy person too, I'll tell you. Being Mother's favorite, she knew this about Jennie and tried to keep her doing things, productive things so's to keep her out of mischief. Mischief like the time she snuck off one sweltering day in August. She was all of about ten years old and she knew the boys were all heading down to the river for a swim. She felt she should be allowed to go too, so when Mother sent her off on an errand, she just kept going. Well Jennie was never very good at lying and when she returned empty-handed after two hours with her hair soaking wet and kinked up all over the place, what could she say?

Trouble was, Jennie didn't see anything wrong with spending the afternoon swimming with the boys in her cotton shift. Too bad Mother didn't agree with her.

No question about it though, she was happiest when she was busy, or maybe she was just less trouble. Mother had her in church groups and she spent a good deal of time trying to teach her to knit, sew and weave. Jennie wasn't much interested in all of that, but she wanted to please Mother in some way, so she tried to stick with it. However, more often than not she was very close to getting in trouble, mostly 'cause of running off with the boys and when those boys got caught doing something wrong, she usually was right there with them.

Farmer Evans once caught a bunch of them in his barn smoking a corncob pipe. No punishment for that mischief was really needed. They all got good and sick and learned their lesson!

Then sometimes when she was supposed to be watching one of our brothers, she'd sweet-talk me so nicely that before you knew what was happening she'd be out the door and I'd be left watching whichever one it was that she'd been left in charge of. Somehow, you just couldn't get mad at her. She was so lively and fun. Actually, she was sweet too and everyone just loved her. Funny though, how she changed so much after she became aware of Jack Skelly.

Well there's more in the telling, and I've written it all down. It's all here, the whole story of how there was only one civilian killed in the Battle at Gettysburg. Took more time than I thought, but it's done now. It's the story of my sister, Jennie Wade.

~ CHAPTER ONE ~

'Suppose the best place to start is that week, the week it all happened. Not hard to remember all the details, they'll be stuck in my mind forever, well most of them anyways. It plays over and over in my mind. There's so many memories, I'd like to forget them all and just pretend it was all a bad dream and go back to the way things were. The way they were before all this happened. That hole in the door though, it keeps it alive. We should probably repair it, but we don't. Not sure if we want to forget the whole thing or remember it forever?

It was 1863, will always remember that, and Lord only knows how long the battles had been going on for. The whole country was fighting. Bad fighting. It must have been at least two years. Too many were getting killed. Both theirs and ours. Ours being the Yanks, anyways that's the side we were supposed to be on. The Confederates were trying to defend what they stood for – slavery and all. We were supposed to be dead set against it but then we weren't farmers and certainly didn't own cotton fields this far north. 'Course my question and the question from most women I knew was how come we can't settle this without killing each other. It wasn't good, but up 'til now it was far away from our sleepy little town.

It was hot, unusually hot, as I recall. Too hot for that time of year in the southern part of Pennsylvania. 'Course I was having a baby about then so I was feeling the weather some. Jennie did everything she could to comfort me. She was about as excited as anyone could be. This being the first baby and all. She'd even decided to move up to my little place, she and Mother that is, and the boys, of course, our three brothers. They were worried, me being alone with no husband. My Louis had been gone for weeks and I'd heard nothing, but I wasn't going to dwell on that. Well, when they all arrived, I'll tell you it wasn't any too soon. It was during that same night when they all moved in that those pains got started. I can recall so well Jennie leaning over me, swiping my forehead with a cool clothe, trying in her sweet way to get me to push.

"Come on Georgie, you can do it. You've got to help here." Then she gave my hand a squeeze and said something like, "C'mon you've always been the brave one." Well that wasn't true, but it wasn't the time to argue the point.

I have no idea in this world how she knew about birthing babies. Never saw it done before as best I can recall. I mean I would've been with her and all if she'd ever seen a baby come into this world.

She was so patient. I told her I couldn't push. I told her how much it hurt. She just said in her sweet way, "I know, I know, but you've just got to try. C'mon, now one good one. This one will be for Louis."

"I am," I nearly yelled. Didn't mean to, it just came out that way. Well she didn't flinch. She didn't flinch either when I grabbed onto her arm and very nearly twisted it off when one of those pains came on me.

"You've always wanted to do that, now haven't you," she said smiling down at me. "And now's your chance, go ahead and break it if you can. You've got a good excuse anyway." It left bruises. I saw my hand print on her wrist the next day, didn't feel any too good about that, but she just ignored it and went about her business.

"Doc's coming soon," she'd said. I know she didn't really believe that, but was just trying to calm me. I mean I'd been laying there for most of the night and there just wasn't much happening except for those pains that were tearing up my insides and wouldn't stop. By the time one had passed and I'd get real comfortable, the next one would be on me. Had no idea it was going to be anything like that.

'Course Harry, our younger brother, was born about eight years ago and I guess we should've learned something about the birthing process, but Mother had sent us away. She said to go on down to the MacGyvers' house and wait there. The Mac-Gyvers were our friends, had been for a long time. They've moved since then, of course. It was the war and all, took too many of them. Miz MacGyver had a hard time of it, ending up with only her old spinster daughter. They moved on up Philadelphia way. Too many memories she said. Had to just get out and leave it all behind.

Kind of a sorry story that was. I mean four sons and a husband? All gone, within a year as I recall. The war: don't think any of us was prepared for the loss and the devastation. They'd left here one by one, those MacGyver boys, and one by one the letters came. First, her second eldest, Randall, killed at Antietam. Then Ben, he had always been a favorite of mine, died in a Reb camp after he'd been taken prisoner. Then Will and Drew, both killed down in Tennessee. Last she heard of her husband was a letter that someone had written for him, that he was badly wounded and in a hospital. That was so many months ago; she just gave up and moved on.

Anyway, at this point you might wonder where our Mother was with all the goings on. Well I guess it would be 'nough said that she didn't do well in situations, if you know what I mean. She'd come by and look down at me and say something about how splotchy my face had gotten and then she'd straighten some imaginary wrinkles on the quilt. The quilt that was, by the way, much too hot for a summer's day in July. But then she'd just make comments about how dusty the room was, ignoring what was taking place. Jennie had asked her as sweet like as she always was, if Mother would be kind enough to entertain Harry and Isaac.

"Mother, they're both going to need some breakfast and then maybe you could get Harry to go on back down and check on Doc Brown. I know he's busy with his doctoring," she'd said, "but sometimes just a bit of a reminder seems to help him along."

Isaac, of course, couldn't go, him being lame and all. Lame since birth actually. Both legs were twisted and misshapen, hardening into crooked limbs of no use. Jennie worked with them sometimes, trying to gently bend them to try to get some use out of them, but they just seemed to get worse. We took care of him a good deal of the time; he was no relation to us. His mother worked and all, she helped out over at the tavern. Isaac had no father. Never bothered to ask why quite frankly. Mother probably knew, but she never talked about such things. So Isaac was a handful, in the true sense of the word. Not to Jennie, of course. She just loved him just the way he was. He couldn't walk a bit. Not one step, not ever. His mother would bring him down to our house in a cart and leave him when she was on her way to work. She'd pick him up most nights. Some nights she just didn't show up. We never worried about her, figured she knew what she was doing.

Anyhow, it seemed that Isaac was happier with us, 'specially with Jennie, if you want the truth of it. His eyes would just light up when she'd come in the room. He called her Miss Jennie, which she once said made her feel old. But she'd heft him up and carry him upstairs and downstairs and in and out of the house, just about anywhere that he wanted to go. On cold days she'd wrap him up in his favorite quilt and set him out on the bench in the sun with his toy soldiers. He just loved it and it was never too much for Jennie. Think maybe she loved that little boy with the lame legs about as much as she loved anyone.

Well anyway, that day I wasn't doing too well. Probably doing more complaining and moaning then was really necessary. Fact is, I was scared, with Jennie knowing next to nothing about birthing babies and with Mother scurrying around all in a twit, trying to maintain some show of order while ignoring the fact that I was about to have a baby. It would've gone much more smoothly if she'd taken the boys down to her own house and just let us be. She did send Harry out to find the doctor though, and he did come home with some news, not much mind you. Took him some time I might add, like it was nearly lunchtime when he got back.

"Doc's tending the sick," he'd said as he slammed the kitchen door. That boy never could come through a door without very nearly tearing it off its hinges. Doc was down with a badly wounded soldier who'd been sent home from the front. Anyhow, that's what he'd said and "he knows that baby's a'comin' and will be up soon enough." That was it. That was all the information that Harry was going to share with us.

"Well," said Mother, "And what of all the soldiers? What did you hear? What did you see? You must've seen something." Then without a pause, she added, "Will you please get that hair out of your eyes."

"Awright," he replied with a scowl, pushing the hair back off his forehead. "I helped a couple of 'em find the store. They're hungry. All of them." And that's as much information as we were going to get out of Harry.

Not my place to say that boy was just plain too sassy, but I'll tell you I wasn't raised that way. Neither was Jennie. That boy just ran around doing pretty much whatever he pleased. Mother would often wring her hands and say she couldn't do a thing with him.

'Course I know she blamed Father for that. They took him away or maybe put him away, Father that is, soon after Harry was born. Mother never told us exactly what happened. Said something like it wasn't for us to know. 'Course I've got my own interpretation of just what went on. I mean, after all, I was there. I was the oldest. I heard things, or I should say I listened when I was supposed to be sleeping. Seems Father took something that didn't belong to him, if you'd really like to know the truth of it. They locked him up. Mother just told us he'd gone away for a while and left it at that.

Well he came home again. Guess it embarrassed Mother some and he started doing crazy things and talking wild so Mother had him carted off again. This time to the Alms House. Haven't seen or heard of him since. Too bad really. He had a nice tailoring business going. After he left it was real hard for Mother to make ends meet, she being just a seam-stress and all. She got paid some for taking in Isaac, but it sure didn't pay the rent.

So by noon that day, it was the 26th of June, how could I ever forget, there was no baby, no doctor and soldiers were wandering about the town. I was about to burst and in about as much pain as a human body could tolerate. It was going to be a long day, I was sure of that and it wasn't going to be much fun for anyone.

~ CHAPTER TWO ~

It was just so hard to imagine what was to come in the next few days. There we were with two little boys and we were three women, one in really hard labor, one just a mite unbalanced and the other trying to keep everything calm. The town was rapidly filling with soldiers, the wrong ones. The Confederates were pouring in, yes pouring in. Have no idea how many but heck, some of them were marching down the street right in front of my house. Some were firing their guns into the air, scaring us all to pieces. It was causing an awful ruckus I'll tell you.

Harry, of course, was wild and just wouldn't stay put. Jennie tried to keep after him but there was just too much else to do. Once he came in to announce that the reason the Confederates were coming into town was 'cause they'd heard tell there was a shipment of shoes that'd arrived and they were stashed somewhere in town just waiting to be taken. Well most of those soldiers were near barefoot; you could see that well enough, so the rumor had some appeal. Never did hear if it was true or not. But there they were. Found out later that when all was said and done, there were close to 80,000 of those Confederate troops in and around our little town that week. Can't say as I know for sure how many actually marched in that day, but I can tell you it was a lot.

Well now Jennie, between trying to keep me calm and the boys happy and Mother out of the way, was busy trying to make a few loaves of bread. "We're going to have to eat you know, war or not, and I'm sure our troops won't be far behind and they'll be looking for something too I'll wager." She had a real practical side to her that more often than not took over when she wasn't off somewhere getting into mischief.

I was doing my best to stay calm and not be too demanding, but it was paining me some just to breathe. Things changed pretty suddenly round about 4 o'clock, and it happened just as the old doc walked through the door. Might I say he arrived not a moment too soon!

Anyway there he was. Huffing and puffing, he was a big man and it was one hot day. His beard, streaked with gray threads, was neatly trimmed, which didn't match his bushy long sideburns. He was always in a rush and liked to knock with one hand and open the door with the other. His footstep was so light you never even heard him moving about and for a man that size, you'd of expected a firmer step. But as he threw open the door, he called out his usual greeting: "Good day ladies, a fine day is it not?"

He was jovial and chatty and as friendly and unconcerned as anyone could ever be. I, on the other hand, had lost some of my good humor as Jennie told it the next day. I was holding on to the bedposts for all I was worth. She said she feared for the bed, afraid I was going to break those posts right off. Guess those deep scratches are from my fingernails. Maybe I should carve in a date, June 26, 1863. I do believe that when the good doctor tried to jolly me a bit, I said a few things that would've been best left unsaid, words that should never have passed from the lips of a lady.

Jennie said she tried as best she could to shush me, but I guess I wouldn't be hushed. She said she finally just put that damp cloth that she'd been using to keep me cool, right smack over my mouth. Can you imagine? Well she said at least that way my conversation was somewhat muffled and hard to understand. Guess I'd managed to raise one of those bushy eyebrows of the old doctor. Probably wondered how I knew such words.

Near about this time, Jennie had Mother go and check the boiling water, said we'd probably need more. It was really anything to get her out of the room. All that Mother had been doing was wringing her hands and pacing around the bed and smoothing the quilt that was keeping me far too warm. She quite frankly looked relieved to have been given a task that would take her elsewhere.

Well that doc just kept chattering on as he brushed crumbs off what had once been his best morning coat. Time and travels had taken their toll on the near threadbare sleeves. He asked about our three brothers and how my husband was doing. Had we heard from him? Hardly listening for an answer, he told us all about the dysentery he'd just treated and the accidental gunshot wound he had to bind up on one of our soldiers who was making his way back to his unit. Not too serious he said. He saw one case of smallpox. "Hope that's going to be the only one, don't need that on top of everything else," he'd said.

Well during all this chatty conversation, he'd be telling me to push. I'm not usually a rude person, but there was the temptation to tell *him* to push. Thought for sure my innards were going to come right out all over that bed. Lord, it hurt bad.

"One more good one Miz McClellan then we'll have it." That's the last I remember him saying 'cause all of a sudden there was this wonderful, high-pitched cry. To this day it brings tears to my eyes just to think of it. And there he was. Tiny beyond description and yelling for all he was worth. Jennie reached over and took him from the doc. Not sure, but it looked like she didn't really trust him to hold on to that tiny little bundle.

She got him all cleaned up while she cooed and talked to him. Got him all quieted down and wrapped in a fuzzy warm blanket, and I swear, if I was a swearing kind of person, and I'm not by nature, 'cept for that day, but by the time she brought him over to me, he was trying to focus his little dark eyes on her face for all he was worth. He was trying so hard to take her in, his smooth little brow furrowed in concentration, trying to remember her for all time, I'm sure. His tiny hand was curled tightly around her outstretched finger, holding on to her and not wanting to let her go.

She seemed reluctant to put him down, like they'd already formed some sort of bond or had a secret that only the two of them knew. Anyhow, she did put him in the crook of my arm and I know to this day that baby's eyes followed her as she moved away from the bed. They say babies can't see; well I know better.

A sweeter more contented little one I've yet to come across. As he was gathering up his things, even Doc Brown said something about what a sweet-tempered child he was going to be. Doc made his apologies and rushed off, saying something about seeing to the little Parker girl with her measles and that I'd be in fine hands with Jennie and Mother to watch over me. He waved at us and said to send Harry on out to get him if we felt we needed him, but he'd be back in the morning to check on us.

'Course he never did come back, what with all the goings on. I wasn't one bit surprised.

Needed to apologize to Jennie for carryin' on so. I'd never done anything like that in my life before and I was just flat-out embarrassed. They called me the quiet one, the studious one. Well after going through that trial, I don't think anyone's ever going to call me the quiet one again. Anyhow told Jennie I was sorry for acting like some Irish washerwoman, but I was truly afraid and just didn't know what to expect.

We had a sister once, they named her Martha, and Mother had a most terrible time birthing her. We were sent away that time for five days. And then look what happened. Baby Martha only lived a few weeks. Sickly from the beginning, not like my baby Louis. He was perky and plump from day one. A better baby I'm sure had never been seen.

His name was actually Louis Kenneth McClellan. Louis after his father. Sure do wish he'd been there. He'd be some proud I can tell you. Anyway thought up the name Kenneth, don't know why just always liked it. Jennie laughed at me some, said I had all that time to think up names and all I chose were girls' names. It's true too. I wanted a girl, in fact knew I was having one. And look what happened! But could I ever change that precious little boy for anything else? Nope. I wouldn't give him up for five little girl babies.

I fell asleep that afternoon with my new sweet bundle, Louis Kenneth McClellan, tucked in my arm. It would've taken more than an army of Confederates to pry that baby loose. He was my precious little one and I was so proud.

~ CHAPTER THREE ~

Guess the passing of that afternoon was anything but typical. To begin with, the day had started bad. The weather was mighty uncomfortable, too humid for words. The sky had been a threatening gray all day, kind of like a huge muffling blanket holding in the heat. There wasn't a breeze or even a ripple to move the heavy air. A feeling of anxiousness surrounded us, almost as though the world had paused, just waiting.

I slept the afternoon away. Just plain out slept, never even woke up until well past sunset. That was when Jennie came in and caught me up on everything. She was flushed from the heat and was patting away all the dampness that had collected on her forehead and cheeks. It'd been a busy afternoon. She said she had no idea how I could've slept through all the noise but she said she'd come in to check on me now and again and I was pretty close to snoring. Baby Louis never even stirred, she'd said. Never could understand how she could've stayed up the entire night before tending to me and then not even catch a catnap.

"Too many things still that need to be done," she'd said. Her biggest task had been to get John James outfitted. He was just 17, younger than both Jennie and I, and like it or not, he had joined the Union Army. Mother was beside herself. Wouldn't even talk about it other than to say if Father were here this wouldn't have happened. So it ended up on Jennie's shoulders to help him out.

You see John James, for whatever reason, was only 5' 3". The smallest in our family except for Harry, but then Harry was only eight and still had some growing to do. So John James needed his uniform drastically altered and Mother being Mother, wasn't going to have anything to do with her son going into the army. Jennie, on the other hand, saw little future for him here in Gettysburg and thought it might just do him a world of good to get out of town, even if the only way was with the army, so she offered to help adjust his uniform. She was a right fine seamstress. Her stitches weren't quite as small as mine and occasionally one could see where she'd veered off a bit, but it was never anything too awfully bad.

It wasn't too long after I fell asleep that she'd gone down to the house on Breckenridge Street. She'd promised him, and she knew John James would be waiting, so she had to go. She said later she was surprised and a little frightened by the Confederates that were still milling about. She said she had an awful feeling of foreboding as she marched herself down the street, but tried to shake it off, and just felt it was lack of sleep that was making her so edgy.

"I was nearly scared out of my wits," she said. "I wanted to run the five blocks down but thought those soldiers may have thought I was up to something." She said she stayed close to the buildings and kept her head down and just moved quickly. Jennie always liked the fellas, there was just no question about that, and I did notice later that she'd changed into her yellow gingham, the one with the pouffy sleeves; it was the one next to her favorite.

She must've had a time I'll tell you, walking down to Breckenridge Street. A few of the Rebs tipped their hats to her and I'll bet she nodded to each of them. She said she tried to keep her eyes down and tried to ignore them without being out-and-out rude. Never mind that they were the enemy and let's have no misunderstandings here, she was in no way a rebel sympathizer, she just enjoyed the attention. Not that her heart didn't belong to Jack Skelly, 'cause it did. I know that for a fact. She was crazy for him but still enjoyed a smile or a nod from a good lookin' fella and I'll tell you that day there were lots of them, anyway lots more than we'd ever seen before.

When she got back that night she did tell me how much they all reminded her of Jack and how she just hoped he would be all right, and if truth be known, she knew it was unlikely that they'd try to detain her. The way she figured it, they weren't going to be overly concerned with one civilian girl off on an errand.

John James was waiting for her when she got down there. She just knew he would be, he relied on Jennie for most everything. In fact she said she was surprised he didn't come up the street looking for her but then he would've been embarrassed carrying his too-big uniform up to my house, the whole world wondering why he wasn't wearing it, and why he wasn't already off with the military. And he would've had to run the gauntlet of all those Confederates and who knows what trouble they were looking for.

So Jennie fitted him up. She said it took some time 'cause that uniform must've been meant for a giant. She said she probably took off enough fabric to make a whole other uniform. Jennie was quick with a pair of scissors, gotta say that. It was done quicker than anyone else could've done it, she was that good.

"That John James," she said, "He was proud as a peacock, he looked right spiffy." He went to be the bugler, you know, with the 21st Pennsylvania Cavalry Regiment. That's what they did with the young ones. He said all through his hitch with the military no one ever believed how old he was, so he just took what they gave him and was proud to be a part of it.

Well he went off, high-tailing it out the back way through town, managing somehow to elude all those Rebs. Never did see baby Louis before he left. Jennie said he asked after the baby and was real sorry that he didn't have time to call, but it would be the first thing he'd do when he got back. He left directly, pounding down the street on that old horse. Said he had to catch up with his unit and all. That group had left just a few hours before the Rebs arrived.

Jennie said that before John James left, he gave her a warning. Seems she was reluctant to tell me, but he'd said we'd all be better off if we'd gotten out of town 'cause there was going to be a terrible battle and we weren't safe. 'Course if we'd wanted to leave town, we should've done it days ago. Now there was just no way that we'd be able to sneak away. We were going to be staying right where we were and just pray that this rumor of a battle was not true.

Jennie said she collected up more things from their house to bring up to my house. She said she didn't mean to take so long, but somehow was feeling a bit nostalgic and took some time walking around her room enjoying the feeling of home. Think maybe that's when she decided to change from her old green dress to the yellow gingham one. She always looked 'specially good in yellow.

There was food to collect too. She'd been making what was known as "war bread," a poor combination of cornmeal, bug-infested flour and water instead of milk. Trying to stretch the few ingredients that were left, had not been easy. We had so little. So she collected every last morsel that they had and brought it up to us. And so like Jennie, she also remembered the toy soldiers that Isaac so dearly loved to play with. So by the time she came trudging back up the hill, her basket was filled to nearly overflowing.

Well, and if you can imagine this, after all she'd been through; on her way back to us she saw a commotion going on in town square. She was curious enough to go on over and have a look to see what it was that was attracting so many of the troops. Well there plump in the middle of the square with all the soldiers surrounding him like some sort of common criminal, was our other brother, Samuel. Big as life, there he was standing in front of some Confederate general!

Just imagine, a general taking the time to deal with our Samuel. Now Samuel was all of about 11 years old at the time. Seems there was some sort of issue about a horse. Well it's never been said that

Jennie was shy when there was an issue she truly believed in so she just marched on up to that table where the general was sitting and asked what it was that was causing them to hold her brother Samuel. She said she was trembling some and tried to keep her voice steady so's they wouldn't know she was frightened.

Well he just answered right back, "Horse thief ma'am."

Jennie did mention that he rose up out of his chair and tipped his hat to her as he said this. They said those southerners were gentlemen, and I'm inclined to believe it, though at that time I'd never met one myself.

Well now that general was all apologetic, but said there just was nothing else he could do. The boy was under arrest and that was that. Jennie protested but he closed the discussion and dismissed her. She was afraid they'd take him somewhere where we'd never see him again, so ran home to tell Mother.

Now Mother has her times, I will give you that, but every now and again she comes through and surprises all of us. This news upset her greatly. After all, she'd entrusted the butcher, Mr. Pierce, with

Samuel's safekeeping. He was to see to him and care for him and board him and, in return, Samuel was to do most of his errands. The arrangement actually worked out quite nicely.

Jennie and Mother had a hard time making ends meet without Father and with Harry to tend to. Taking in little lame Isaac produced a bit of an income and then Jennie and Mother took in sewing and all, trying to keep up what once was a fine tailoring business. But it was very hard, making ends meet, so Samuel ended up at the butchers almost like indenture, but of course they didn't do indenture anymore. He seemed to like it well enough; he never complained that I knew of.

So Mother, very nearly in a fit of temper, partly because butcher Pierce wasn't properly tending to Samuel and partly because the entire day had been most distracting, set out for town square. By herself, I might add. Not like her at all. She'd become somewhat shy over the years and really preferred to just stay indoors and let others tend to the errands and such. Well, she slapped her bonnet on her head, not her best mind you. She would've had to go home to get that one. But this was her second best, the one with that teeny pink rose on the side, with the little green leaves sticking out at odd angles. She marched on down there, and if you can believe it, came back up that hill with Samuel in tow.

Never did say too much of just what went on, or that it was General Jubal A. Early that she talked to. Didn't mean much to us at the time, but when my Louis got home and we told him all about the goings on, he was some impressed. He said that General Early, known for his occasional bad temper, was in charge of a good part of the Rebel forces. So Samuel was just plain out lucky to have gotten out of whatever mischief he'd been up to.

It took awhile but slowly we were able to drag bits and pieces out of him. None of my brothers by the way were ever much good at sharing information. Anyways it seems that the butcher had a prize horse, or so the butcher said. More'n likely it was his only horse, if you get my meaning. But he had this horse that he prized, let's put it that way. Well he asked Samuel to take it on out of town before it was stolen or impounded by the troops. He said soldiers from either side could just help themselves to his horse if they so choose.

Samuel's a good boy and pretty much does what he's told, and if you want my opinion, he likes a bit of adventure now and again. Being that he was too young to join the army, this was as close as he was going to get to high adventure. Well he saddled up that old mare and he got out of town before anyone even knew it. He said he was going to try to get that horse over to Mitchell's farm, quite a few miles north of where he was.

Now, I've been there once or twice in the buggy, and I can tell you it's a trip, at least four hours of bad road that washes out every time we have a storm. Didn't ask him how he was going to get back. Figured he knew that for himself and wasn't interested in sharing that information with me. So, he headed out of town in one fired-up gallop. Didn't get far. That's the sorry part of this whole business. He hadn't even gotten out to the Baltimore Pike when they caught up with him. Needless to say those Rebs now have themselves a fine horse, and after that, Samuel spent a mighty long time hiding out in the butcher's cellar.

Seems that was the deal that Mother struck with the general: "Get this boy out of my sight and keep him out of my sight and we'll overlook this whole thing."

Mother I guess threatened Samuel with the switch across his bottom if she so much as saw one hair on his head until the town was completely cleared of all those "horrid" Rebel soldiers. "Just look what they're doing to our town." At this point, she was nearly in tears.

As it was, Jennie had to sneak him down to the butcher's just after sunset so's he could hide out in the cellar. And if you're looking for the truth of the whole thing and I sort of promised Samuel I'd keep this to myself, but it's a kick so find myself sharing it now and again. Remember how Jennie brought up those extra clothes? Well, she had this fine light blue lawn dress. It had the daintiest little sprigged bluebells all over it and a fine lace collar. You can imagine what she did! That dress and her old straw bonnet, the one that she used when she'd help farmer Driscoll pick apples, it really wasn't in the best of shape, but it'd do in a pinch. It was a sight. Couldn't laugh that hard in my condition and all, but it was one of the highlights of that day to see Samuel in his disguise walking down to the butcher's shop. He was scowling and about as unhappy as one can get, with his long arms hanging out of the dress, looking at Jennie as if she were the enemy. Mother chimed in that he was to do what he was told, that he didn't want to risk being caught.

That dress couldn't have been more perfect. Matched his eyes it did, and I told him so too, which just put him into a fit of scowling. Good thing Harry wasn't there to see it. That would've been the end of Samuel's fine reputation with his friends, not that Harry would blab about everything, but that sight would've just been too much for him to keep to himself.

Anyhow, Jennie walked him down to make sure he got there. She came back carrying the basket that she'd made Samuel carry so's he'd look more girl like and could sort of hide his big hairy hands and raggedy fingernails.

She said he was the worst looking girl she'd ever seen, bar none. I said something like, "you mean worse than spinster Fitzpatrick?" can't be that bad. Now there was no call to go saying that but I did. She said he looked even worse than that. The dress kept getting caught up cause he wouldn't take his trousers off and it kept catching on the wool fabric and wrapping around his legs. It took her two steps to keep up with his stride and he just wouldn't slow down. Well anyway, the deed was done and as far as we knew he stayed put in the butcher's cellar. We did not see hide nor hair of him 'til we had to send for him later, 'cept when Jennie snuck down. But that's another story.

Anyhow, things didn't calm down that night 'til well after midnight what with getting Louis Kenneth changed and fed and settled down. Jennie went out to get water just one last time and she said it was eerie, you could see all the campfires from the Confederate troops all up the side of South Mountain. Must've been a passel of them 'cause that mountain's miles away.

It felt sort of like the whole world had paused. There were no owls that night or spring peepers. It seemed like even the neighborhood dogs had taken a break. I shivered as I pulled the quilt up to hold out the night air.

~ CHAPTER FOUR ~

Just imagine, more than 85,000 Union troops descending on a town of a mere 2,400 people. Well that's what happened and it wasn't any too soon either, I'll tell you with all those Reb troops threatening to come down on us. They'd been holed up already a couple of days and every household was strained to the limit. I think the Rebs raided all those outlying farms, one after another, of just about everything they had. We heard later that they had emptied the larders of every farmhouse within miles. There wasn't a dried apple or stored winter potato left. In fact, it was early for peaches, but they were eating those hard little nuggets right off those trees.

Now those Union troops actually came in toward evening on June 30. It was a Tuesday as I recollect and I wasn't quite on my feet yet, but Harry, good as always at being everywhere at once, saw them march into town up by Emmitsburg Road. He said people actually gathered and cheered them on as they came down the road. Well Jennie was ready. She'd been baking bread for a couple of days. There were some perfectly rounded loaves and a few baskets of biscuits neatly lined up with a clean napkin thrown over them. Flies were a constant bother during the summer months and this year they seemed peskier than usual.

Anyone who passed by and looked even a bit hungry was welcome to whatever she had. She would turn no one away. The word must've been passed about the pretty girl up on Baltimore Street, 'cause I'll tell you, there was a steady stream of those ragged blue uniforms, even into the night, it was as if a floodgate had been opened up.

Lying abed in the next room, it was easy to hear the chatter as one after another came to the door looking for something to eat. Some were mighty funny with their flirting and all. I'm sure Jennie loved it. At least five different times one of the soldiers had said how much she reminded him of his sister. Think maybe they just wanted to get her to talk to them. She asked a few if they'd ever met up with one Jack Skelly. They all said no, hadn't met him yet.

I knew he was on her mind. You could tell because she kept fingering that picture of him that she kept in her apron pocket. I knew it was there 'cause once she showed it to me and every once in awhile you could see a corner of it when she bent over the bed while she tended to Louis Kenneth. She also kept his last letter tucked up in the bodice of her dress. When she spent the night in my room after Louis was born I saw her reading it over and over and then tucking it back next to her heart.

Anyway, after the Unions arrived, we knew there was going to be trouble. Jennie had spent the last few nights down at Mother's house. She'd told me she went down that evening to check on Samuel down in the butcher's cellar. Always watchful of everyone, she was afraid he wasn't going to get enough to eat so she brought him some biscuits and cornbread. She said she was a mite nervous as there were all those Rebel sharpshooters sitting up in the windows. Even though you couldn't see them, it was easy to see where they were 'cause the light reflected off their gun barrels.

Jennie said she tried to act real casual and pretend like she was just making a delivery to the butcher. She said she wanted to get Samuel something to drink too, so she pulled up a bucket of water from that well he's got out back and just sort of stood there casually drinking from the dipper, trying to figure out what to do next. Well and wouldn't you know, just at that moment a shot rang out.

"Now Georgie," she said, "It took my heart a couple of moments to get back into my chest. You can't imagine the fright, but then I made a dash for the cellar. I figured that shot would keep their attention, and just thanked my stars it hadn't been aimed at me."

Anyway she safely made it to Samuel and he was some glad to see her. He's almost 12 and he's one that likes the company of others and was getting a mite lonely even though he'd snuck out the night before. Mother never knew that, thank heavens. She would've come down and tanned his bottom, old as he was and all. Well he told Jennie that last night he'd heard the soldiers talking and there was going to be a fray and it was going to be a big one. He said he stood in an alley down by Frazier's blacksmithing shop, and heard some of the Confederates talking about the shoes that they'd come for, but so far no one had been able to find any sign of a shipment of shoes. And now all the Yanks had arrived so there was going to be some big trouble.

It certainly sounded worrisome. Anyhow, we couldn't share this with Mother 'cause we didn't want her to know that anyone had even seen Samuel. Jennie said she was real glad that she'd gotten down there to check on him. He seemed so lonely, and if need be she'd go on back down there again.

Well anyway, Jennie'd decided that she'd stay in her own home. It was more comfortable for her and the two boys, Isaac and Harry. Mine was so small. I knew that. We were only renting half of the double house. There was another family on the other side and mine was awfully small what with only one bedroom upstairs and only the sitting room and kitchen down and my bed was now taking up most of the space in the sitting room.

Mother and Jennie had decided that moving that big four poster bed, would make life a whole lot easier, and might I say cooler, as that attic could take the breath right out of you on a hot summer day. So I had quickly agreed, I'd be able to stay right next to the kitchen until I could be up on my feet again. It was early in the spring when I let them all carry my bed down with my feather puff and pillows and got everything settled into the sitting room. It was ever so much more comfortable and a nicer place to be, right smack in the middle of all the goings on.

Well anyway, that night Jennie went home just knowing trouble was in the air. Sure enough the next morning not too long after sunrise, we heard the first shots. It was frightening to say the least. Not much we could do but stay put. Couldn't be hiding in the cellar, 'cause we'd have to go outside to get to the entrance and it was too dangerous and I still wasn't walking so good. We decided we were better off right where we were. Jennie had walked back up from her house even before the morning light and when we heard those shots she decided she had best go back down and get the boys. Isaac, she was sure, would be frightened out of his very wits and Harry would probably be out getting into some mischief and she somehow was going to have to try to restrain him. I didn't think it was a good idea, but it was asking for trouble to leave a crippled child and a boy alone, one that was always itching to get into mischief.

Jennie traveled down that hill twice to bring them up. She couldn't find the handcart that we most times used to transport Isaac with his little lame legs, so she ended up carrying him by herself. It was hot out there and guns were going off and it was just bedlam all around, with smoke and noise and people and soldiers running about. The confusion and screams outside my window about unnerved me.

Well who knows how but she got both those boys up the hill. They arrived in my room nearly speechless, their eyes so wide I thought they'd pop. There was nothing to do but settle them on the floor under my bed. They were more than glad to crawl under with their toy soldiers. They didn't do much playing but would just peek out with every new round of gunshots. They seemed as settled as they were going to be so Jennie left them to me and was back out there handing out water to the soldiers.

And that's just about how she spent the entire day as one after another stopped to either fill their canteen or have a cup of cool water. It was such a relief I'm sure for those Union troops as they marched into battle to have that pretty girl standing at the side of the road passing out all the water they wanted. Not only were they thirsty but hungry and tired too I imagine.

The chaos, the noise, the heat, it was unending. The air got so heavy with the stench of hot metal and fiery explosives that it left you panting for a breath of uncluttered air. The noise was near deafening. I wanted to pull my pillow over my head and somehow block it all out.

It wasn't more than a few hours later that they changed direction. Just like that. I could see it out my window. They were heading the other way; things weren't looking good if you know what I mean. Seemed like those Rebel troops were in hot pursuit. Battle weary, some wounded, some being carried, they ran, walked and limped past our house. Jennie just kept handing out water to anyone that wanted it. She must've filled near a thousand canteens that day. There were so many injuries and most of the uniforms were tattered or in shreds. There were jackets without sleeves, trousers without legs, hats that seemed to be there only to catch the running blood. It's just hard to imagine and hard to remember the horror of it all.

How had she kept up with it? By late day her skirt was dirty and soaked through and she'd just plain gone and worn a path through the grass from the street back to the well. Those soldiers were so grateful I'll tell you.

Mother was nearly beside herself with fear and just plain demanded that Jennie get back in the house. Over across the way at Rupp's Tannery some Rebel troops had just gone and made themselves comfortable in the windows of the building and were taking shots over this way. Even Jennie saw the foolishness of staying out there. She came back in and worked at comforting the two boys.

Fearless Harry at eight years old had chosen to just stop speaking and with each new barrage of bullets he threw his small grubby hands over his eyes. He thought he could disappear that way I'm quite sure. Jennie had to coax him out from under the bed and then she held him in her lap for a good half hour to try to calm him. While she sat there I got up with or without her permission and went and found a salve for her hands. They were badly blistered from lugging that pail of water back and forth from the well. The open sores on her palms were weeping and must've been painful.

With a bit of coaxing, the two boys agreed to slide back under the bed. Jennie pushed a couple of pillows under to keep them comfortable thinking maybe they'd even fall asleep. Not the easiest thing with what was going on outside. It didn't sound like it was going to stop anytime soon.

The crackle of gunfire and the shattering boom of cannons seemed some distance away, but still it felt like they were fired under our windows. The air was filled with the stench of gunpowder and the smoke and screams of men was nearly unbearable. You just wanted to cover your eyes and ears and hold your nose to cut out the horror of the sights and sounds that were everywhere. How could anyone ever forget it?

I tried to get back up and help some. I thought to make dinner for everyone, but Jennie pushed me back down and said no such-a-thing was going to happen while she still took a breath. Reluctantly I did as I was told. I was not one to lay about all day and it was truly upsetting me to watch everyone busy at work while I just lay there like a slug-a-bed. Jennie said soon enough I'd be up and doing it all, but for now I needed to get my strength back and tend to Louis.

There was always mending to do and she did hand me a basket of what needed doing. I know she was trying to get me interested in something besides all the goings on. "Here," she said, "Your stitches have always been finer than mine and you know what a stickler Annie Adamson is about her clothing," and gave me a knowing look as she handed me the green serge dress.

This was supposed to distract me and it did for a bit. Jennie and Mother were seamstresses and always had more work than they could handle. I was glad to help especially with Annie Adamson, because she always gave Jennie a time, I'll tell you.

We'd all been in school together and that Annie could certainly lord her wealth over everyone. And she was finicky! Seemed there wasn't much that pleased that girl or maybe she just liked to hear herself complain. Anyhow Jennie let me worry about letting out that girl's Sunday dress, again. While everyone else wasn't getting enough to eat with the war and all, seemed like Annie had been putting on more weight. This was the third time we'd let that dress out. Not my place to talk, but maybe the divine Miss Adamson should start thinking of a husband, if you know what I'm saying here.

Anyway, I laid propped up in bed trying my best to concentrate but actually doing little if anything. Seemed that every stitch I took was a little tighter than the last and the whole seam had started to pucker badly. Jennie was in the kitchen banging about with spoons and pots. I had the feeling her motive was to drown out the sounds from outside. And it wasn't too long before she had somehow put together food for all of us. I have no idea at all where she came up with the ingredients. There was a crock full of rich dark baked beans, and a pan of scrumptious corn bread slathered with bacon drippings. There was even cold cider, watered down some, but nevertheless the flavor of last fall's apples was still there. It was like a king's feast, there'd been so little for so long.

She'd made extra she said, knowing full well there would be men who would be knocking on our door. And as it happened Jennie had just sat down when a knock came. He said something like, "Ma'am I heard you all had bread. If it wouldn't be too much trouble would it be possible to get a piece or two for those fighting for the Union ma'am?"

He'd added the last almost as an afterthought. I watched as Jennie took the cornbread right off her plate and gave it to him.

"There you go now soldier," she'd said. "We're happy to share and only too glad to help." She came back in and I told her I would not eat one more bite until she took my bread too and gave it to the next soldier that knocked on the door. I just wasn't going to stuff myself full while others went hungry. And sure enough there were many more who came by.

It was well after dark before everything got cleaned up and we all got settled down. The two boys slept under my bed on their quilts. Harry slept fitfully tossing about and Isaac was just fine as long as he had his special quilt. Jennie had made sure that she brought it up from the other house. He was some attached to that quilt. It was the one that was once spread on Mother's bed, but since Father left, Mother hadn't wanted it on her bed. She never explained, but just removed it and had it folded up in the old pine chest until Isaac came along and discovered it. He loved it. It was so worn, its edges frayed, always shedding pieces of thread. Isaac liked the colors; it was a kaleidoscope of shapes that all seemed to somehow go together in one great pattern.

Mother had pieced it all together shortly after she was married. She'd put in scraps of fabric from her cotton lace wedding dress, from the old blue shirt that Father had worn the day they were married and from a few of her dresses from when she was a young girl. It was worn and faded and mended in spots but it was Isaac's favorite and he found great comfort in sitting or lying on it when he was at the Mother's house.

Well that night, Mother never even undressed, she was so sure we were going to be raided while we slept and so she just laid right down next to me in my bed. The last to turn in, Jennie tried to get comfortable on top of the chaise under the two windows. She too refused to take off her dress and put on her night shift. With the sounds of the random bullets flying back and forth outside, I believe they were right.

It was a night I'll tell you, soldiers were groaning and crying out from their wounds, along with the occasional scream of someone hurt really bad. The bullets were being fired just often enough to discourage any sleep at all. It was dreadful and nearly unimaginable in our small town. Baby Louis slept through it all.

~ CHAPTER FIVE ~

The night was so hot and close. Our room was stifling: five people and one baby all sleeping in a hodgepodge of arms and legs and quilts and pillows. It was near impossible to even close my eyes. Not sure if it was the frightening sounds from outside or that I'd been abed for nearly a week and was just plain fidgety. In any case Mother slept fully clothed right next to me. She'd snore quietly now and again and I was glad that she could find some peace in sleep.

The two boys were under the bed on their quilts. I think they truly felt safer there, where some of the sounds were muffled. Jennie lay on the chaise, her head resting on a very small pillow. You could tell she was exhausted. She'd been caring for all of us for over a week and tending to all the soldiers that came to the door. Dark circles were etched under her eyes and the usual good humor that had never failed her was wearing thin. She was tired, and more than any of us, needed a good night's sleep.

I watched as she read a few pages of scripture by the light of the candle. I wonder now if she knew something or felt something that we weren't aware of.

In any case, she dozed fitfully through the night. A furrow in her brow seemed to deepen with the passing hours. She was so still, I was afraid she might roll over and slide right off that chaise, but I had no need to be worried. Although her breathing was irregular and once she cried out, she stayed almost perfectly still lying on her back.

Baby Louis stirred and needed to be fed. I took care of everything keeping as quiet as possible, glad that for once Jennie didn't jump up to help. When I'd finished with Louis and he was all tidy and snug, I tucked him back in his cradle. As quietly as I could, I crept over to Jennie and blew out her candle.

Sleep just wouldn't come when I saw her sit up and look around as though trying to remember where she was. She was trying to shake off the drowsiness. The sky was beginning to show the colors of the coming day when a mourning dove began to stir, calling out his lonesome tune. I hadn't heard a gunshot in a few hours. I saw Jennie lean over to pull on her shoes and then watched as she crept across the room, through the door and into the kitchen.

The usual morning sounds broke through the unnatural silence as she scraped the hearth, trying to find a spark to bring the fire back to life. There was more to do than she'd be able to handle alone, so she crept back in and jiggled Harry awake. He needed to help out and carry in some wood so that she could get something prepared for all of us.

Harry isn't the most willing worker there is, but he'll most times do what you ask without too much of an argument. So he crawled out from under the bed and I heard him go out three different times to collect wood from out back. And Jennie was right there catching the door each time he came in. What was it about Harry and door slamming? It would wake the dead every time it closed behind him.

Well he had a fine stack next to the hearth and Jennie told him he could go back to bed. Then she went and fetched water. The dark was still so thick I could see the glow from her lantern out my window. After two trips to the well, she crept in and saw that I was awake.

"Good morning to you sister," she'd whispered, "could I bring you something, tea or water perhaps?" I'd refused. Said I'd wait for the others to get up when we could have breakfast together. Mother was stirring a little, the boys however hadn't moved since Harry had crept back under the bed.

Straightening out my covers and already looking harried, she said, "There are so many soldiers out there, some so very badly wounded. I don't know what can be done. I spoke to some of them, they're in such pain." She shook her head as though not knowing what to do. Turning abruptly she said she'd get something together for us to eat and would then go outside to see what she could do to help.

Before the sun was even up, there'd been bread rising in the big wood dough trough, she wouldn't stop. I could hear the door closing almost without a sound between the kitchen and the outside. Every time she had a free minute she was bringing water to the wounded soldiers. They were scattered around our yard like the fallen leaves of autumn, browned by frost and blown about. Later she told me how so many were so badly injured, she had to help them to raise their heads so that they could drink.

When she came to bring the tea, whether I wanted it or not, I could tell she was upset. Trying to hold the tears back she told me the story of how she'd tried to help one very young soldier. He couldn't have been more than 16 or 17, maybe younger, but she didn't even want to think about that. She'd tried to help him with a drink of water, but he'd had such a bad neck wound that she couldn't raise his head. She said she was quite sure that she recognized him as one of the soldiers that had come for bread. He'd tried to talk to her and tell her where he was from. Jennie said she could barely understand him, he was in such agony. She thinks he was from Albany, way up in New York. He begged for a drink, she said there were tears in his eyes as he mouthed the word thirsty. She tried to lift his head just a bit to get some water to him and as she cradled his head with one hand with blood seeping from his wound and between her fingers, he gave one last gasp and breathed no more.

She was so upset. We didn't want to wake everyone so I just held her as we whispered back and forth. I didn't know what to tell her so just said something like it wasn't her fault that he was gone. Think that's what she wanted to hear. Think maybe she thought she'd done something wrong that'd caused his death. She hadn't.

I wanted to somehow try to make sense of this war for her, somehow try to put it into words and explain it. But how? I said something like they're fighting for the freedom of the slaves, or some such, but I had to question this terrible carnage, even as I said it. She asked how can they go about killing each other. Aren't we all Americans and they're all so young? Do they even know what this is all about? She shook her head as if trying to understand something that was just plain beyond reason.

I was at a loss and could only assure her that the boy who had just died had a wound so bad there was absolutely nothing that anyone could've done and she'd done the right thing by talking to him and trying to comfort him in his final moments. It calmed her some, but there was a sadness etched around those dark eyes that I'd never seen before. In a fleeting moment, I wondered if it'd ever go away or would she forever more be marked by the strain showing in her once-merry face. With great effort, she pulled herself up, wiped her eyes with a corner of her splattered apron and returned to the kitchen.

The sun had been up awhile before the two young boys crawled out from their protected shelter. Mother had gotten up at that point and was fussing around in the kitchen trying to help Jennie. By the time the boys were fully awake she had Mother bringing us the last of the oatmeal with just a spatter of milk. She continued with her bread-making tasks. I'd fed baby Louis again and found myself getting just plain fidgety to the point that I would no longer listen to anyone. I was going to get up no matter what they all said. So while Jennie and Mother were busy in the kitchen, I just up and left my bed and sat in the rocker next to Louis' cradle. Guess I was a bit lightheaded, 'cause I didn't get to that rocker any too soon. It was so nice to be sitting up and out of that bed.

Wouldn't you know, Jennie came in and had a proper fit. "What do you think you're doing? Whatever would Doc Brown say if he saw you?" and on and on. I let her say her piece, then reminded her that chances were slim that we'd see the good doctor again anytime soon and besides, I felt just fine and if I had to stay in that bed one more minute I was positively going to have a fit.

Jennie said something like, "Suit yourself, you always were the stubborn one." But she smiled as she said it and reached down for baby Louis who by this time was squalling with his cheeks all puffed out and his little face turning bright red. He was making his own fine racket in the ruckus that had been going on around him.

She cuddled him some to settle him down before she handed him over. She did love that baby, no question about that, and he certainly seemed to have something for her 'cause whenever she held him he'd look right up at her, crinkling his beautiful little brow, trying to focus on his Aunt Jennie. She was so sweet and kind with him, it was wonderful to watch. Well I ended up promising to get back into bed and nap twice a day until Doc Brown came and gave me permission to go about my regular tasks. She smiled, saying she'd known all along I wouldn't last in bed a full two weeks. If nothing else, it was awfully good to see her a bit cheerful again.

Jennie spent most of that day back outside quietly going among the soldiers and passing out water and then bread. It seemed that every time she came back into the house, there'd be another knock on the door with soldiers begging something to eat. We just marveled at how popular Jennie's "war bread" was. It was made with whatever ingredients she could find. She said it was the poorest bread ever made. In fact, she thought it was so bad she probably wouldn't have even fed it to the chickens.

Now if you really want the truth of the matter she was quite the baker, so this must have pained her some to be serving it. Her best bread was really something to behold. She'd add just a teaspoon of sugar, and just a smidgen of nutmeg, her magic ingredients. That bread was a treat. It was so good. It was really something special, even more so when it came warm from the oven. But there was no sugar to be found anymore and certainly no nutmeg left. Only coarse corn meal remained, with very little left of the fine ground wheat flour.

There was such a steady stream of hungry soldiers that she couldn't keep up with them. She'd asked some to wait just a bit and she'd even asked a few to step inside while she finished slicing off a piece or taking the biscuits out of the brick oven. Later she'd said that she'd tried to ignore all their flirting as she continued her work at the hearth, but they all wanted to help.

They were in such bad shape, even I could see, that. Some without shoes, their uniforms in tatters and dirty beyond description. But Jenny'd smile as they offered to take up the wood peel and slide the freshly baked bread out of the brick oven. She gave them a shy glance and said no, that was all right, she had to load some coals back into it to get it piping hot again and it needed just the right amount, so she'd be fine, thank you anyway.

Isaac was sitting on the stairs that led up to the second floor. He was wide-eyed and about struck dumb seeing all the soldiers filing in and out with their rifles so casually slung over their shoulders. He wanted more than anything to go sit outside among them, but Jennie said that wouldn't be wise, so instead she'd let different ones in to wait just a moment while she finished slicing or removing the freshly baked biscuits or bread. They were all so sweet and kind. They would look over and see the little crippled boy and would try to befriend him. He was so shy and in such awe of all those bigger-than-life soldiers standing right there in front of him that he could only manage an occasional nod.

A tall gangly one, thin beyond description with a uniform in near tatters, gave him a small knife that he said he took from a dead Reb in Vicksburg. Another, with a cheery smile, gave him a package of hardtack, "should you ever be caught outside with nothing to eat," he said. "Don't eat it though son unless you're near to starving." He laughed, "It's that bad."

Isaac grinned from ear to ear, the dark space where he'd lost his front tooth looking like a great gaping hole. It was better than if someone had given him a handful of shiny gold pieces, he was so proud of that package of hardtack and that little knife.

We were getting real close to running out of just about everything. We'd had enough stores put by to last us 'til the summer vegetables started coming in, but with all the bread and biscuits that Jennie had passed out we were quickly running out of nearly all our supplies. As it was, Jennie was using the last of the flour that the grocer had sold to us just last week. He sold it to Jennie for not much money 'cause he said the bugs had gotten to it. Well let me tell you, he had no idea how many of those bugs had gotten to it! Jennie said that as she measured it out, she spent nearly five minutes with each cup picking out the weevils. Finally she had Isaac busy doing it and he was happy to help. With his small fingers and sharp eyes he was both nimble and quick.

He adored Jennie, practically worshiped her actually, so he'd do just about anything she asked. And as for those little bugs, we would've fed them to the chickens 'cept there were no chickens. Jennie had announced that morning that the chickens were gone. She'd found the last four eggs that they'd laid, but those old hens were long gone. Either the noise of the guns had scared them into the next county or the Rebs had stolen them for the stew pot. Regardless, we were down to our last four eggs.

By afternoon I was back in bed. The day was hot and heavy and everything felt damp with the heat. Seemed like I was more tired than I knew, so I was happy to follow Jennie's orders and crawl back in. Isaac was comfortably curled up under the bed for an afternoon nap. There was still so much going on it was best that he was out of the way. Now Harry was another story. Every once in a while he'd stick his head in the kitchen door and announce to Jennie that he was off doing more errands for the troops, and then before she could object the door would slam shut and he'd be off again.

The missile hit around 4 o'clock. No warning at all. Just an odd whistling sound through the air. It very nearly blew up the entire house and about scared us to death. There was a horrible, ear–splitting crash, followed by a rain of bricks crashing down. We'd heard bullets being fired all day by the sharpshooters, but this ear-splitting boom was terrifying and so unexpected. It shook the house to its very foundation.

Imagine listening to bricks raining down just above our heads. We truly thought the house was going to come down around us, that this was the end; they'd find us buried under the rubble. Jennie had been in the kitchen mixing up yet another batch of bread. The boom was so startling and frightening, she fainted dead away. Imagine our shock when Mother called out to her and got no answer. She jumped up and tried to push open the door between the two rooms but couldn't 'cause Jennie was lying there, blocking the door.

Fearing something dreadful had happened, I got up, ignoring what Mother had to say about my condition. Between the two of us we pushed that door open partway and found Jennie there on the floor in a dead faint. Mother screamed, and then screamed again, a high pitched frightening sound. She thought sure Jennie was dead. With all that screaming it brought Jennie around as well as got the attention of all the soldiers outside. I found a towel and wet it and held it to her forehead. She looked up at me a bit dazed, wondering what she was doing on the floor with me looking down at her.

First thing she did was reach into her apron pocket. I knew what she was checking for. You could see the outline of her fingers holding that little portrait of Jack Skelly. A peace came across her face as she held that little daguerreotype. She sure did have some strong feelings for that boy. Didn't talk that much about him, but you knew, you could just tell.

Anyhow, the door flew open and soldiers came pouring into the kitchen. We were packed so tight I didn't think Jennie would get any air at all. We sat her up on a stool and gave her sips of water 'til she was back to being herself. Think she was embarrassed some by all the commotion.

"Oh Georgie, I'm just fine," she said, "Now leave me be and you go on and get back in that bed." Well if you want my opinion, I think she'd fainted dead away 'cause there were just too many sleepless nights and too much worry for one body to take and it just plain caught up to her. Jennie was not the type that just fainted away at every little thing.

Well, let me tell you, those soldiers were mighty nice. I imagine some of them saw that missile hit and parts of that roof probably rained down on them. They offered to go on upstairs and fix whatever it was that needed repair and see if the house was all right.

They all went up. I stayed down with Isaac. Once again, Harry was off somewhere. Imagine his disappointment when he returned. He'd missed all the excitement. Well all those soldiers trooped back down the stairs. Lord, there must have been a dozen or more. First thing they said was that we were danged lucky that shell hadn't exploded like it was supposed to 'cause we'd all be in kingdom come. They said just leave it be. Later though, that roof was going to need patching.

That missile had made a huge hole in the wall between my half of the house and my neighbor Miz McClain's half. She was a widow, you know. Sorry business that. Four children, all under 10 years old and just the month before her husband had been killed. Don't know of a sorrier tale. It wasn't right, they were the nicest family. Mr. McClain had been such a good father to those four precious children. Still makes me sad to think of those fatherless babes. Anyhow, they weren't home, they'd gone up to be with Miz McClain's sister up north somewhere. As far away as they could get from this war, Miz McClain had said as she packed all their belongings on the back of a borrowed farm wagon. Haven't heard from her since.

Anyway that unexploded shell had gone through our wall and was on the floor of her attic. Jennie said it was still smoking when she got there. The soldiers said that not much could be done about the wall, but they'd tend to patching up the roof. If you want my opinion, if we hadn't had pretty Jennie with us, with her tiny waist and her big brown eyes, that roof probably would've been left, but they were happy to help. Think we had more of them working up there than was truly necessary, but they all seemed to be enjoying each other's company so much. It couldn't have taken more than a half hour. I guess there was such horror and misery and pain and suffering right outside our kitchen door, they were relieved to have something else to do.

Looked to me like every time another soldier appeared at the door Jennie would reach in her pocket and touch that picture. Maybe she was saying a silent prayer that someone was watching over him, that he'd be kept out of harm's way.

In any case when she finally stretched out on the chaise late that night I saw her once again reach into the top of her dress and pull out that well-worn letter, the last one he'd written. She must've had it memorized because it was well worn by now what with the dampness and being unfolded so many times.

As we all laid there thinking our own thoughts, a soldier out in the yard started playing his harmonica. And what a sad and mournful tune it was; "Home Sweet Home." The tune warbled through the dark, its melancholy sound carried by the breeze through the welcome quiet of the darkness.

We all fell into a fitful sleep while the moon tried to shine its light through the gray blanket of smoke that covered the land. It cast a dull glow that seeped ghostlike through our windows.

~ CHAPTER SIX ~

Louis was much like our old rooster, the one who liked to sound his wake up call to let us know it was time to rise and shine. He wasn't a light sleeper, but he did start fussing nearly every four hours and he woke us all up early, before the sun was even up. Anyways he woke Jennie and me. Mother slept on. She was lying right next to me, but she could somehow sleep the sleep of the dead and she would just snore on. Jennie jumped up the minute Louis began to stir; she was still after me about staying in bed. I won some of the arguments but she won more and whenever she could she'd be up and insist that I lie there. She got to Louis quicker than I could and lifted up that tiny precious bundle and cleaned his nappies and got him all settled down before she handed him to me all sweet smelling and fresh.

While I fed him, Jennie sat on the side of my bed and we talked quietly, mostly about the war as I remember. We were both so tired of it and wondered whether it would ever end and if we would ever see our friends and loved ones again. I was feeling particularly lonely at that moment for my husband Louis. We really hadn't been married all that long before he up and left and now I hadn't heard from him in so long. Wasn't even sure where he was, and just prayed he was safe and not going through something like what was going on right outside our window. He didn't even know about his new son. As always, Jennie tried to lighten my mood especially when the tears threatened to spill. Don't worry she'd said, he'd be just fine and I'd hear from him soon enough. I needed to put all my strength into caring for the baby.

She'd been toying with that tortoise shell comb that she loved so much and started to drag it through that hopeless mop of curls of hers. Try as she might in smoothing back a tidy bun, those flyaway curls were giving her fits. Whatever she managed to tuck up out of the way, I knew it wouldn't be for long, especially in the hot humid air; soon enough there'd be escaping curls everywhere. Anyway, she decided to put on the one clean dress she'd brought up from Breckenridge Street because her other one was just a sight and she wasn't going to wear it another day. So she pulled on her blue cotton and took the clean apron from behind the door. I pretended not to notice when she switched the picture from one pocket to the other and how she removed that letter into the bodice of the clean blue cotton. She saw me smiling by the light of the candle, but then just patted her pocket and had her own private smile. She turned and disappeared into the kitchen.

I heard her scraping back the ash from last night's cook fire and put a few twigs on the embers to get the breakfast fire going. It was going to be hot in that kitchen with little air passing through. She left the door ajar when she went out to get water and wood. It took her an unusually long time, but when she came back into my room with fresh tea, she'd said that there were just too many of them. Her eyes were about as sad as I'd ever seen them. There were injured soldiers everywhere; she wondered aloud what she could do.

"I tried," she'd said. The tears started to flow as she told of the conversations she'd had with a few of them. It was confusing in the dark, she'd said with only a few lanterns lit. There were bodies everywhere, sitting, lying, some curled up tight into a protective ball. Their wounds and suffering were terrible.

One soldier she said had been so gravely injured she knew there was no hope. He had only a bloody stump of an arm. His shirt had been ripped off with only a collar remaining tightly buttoned around his neck. He had such warm and caring young eyes she said. She sat next to him for just a moment to offer him water. They chatted quietly for a bit and when she asked where he was from, he'd said Charleston, way down in South Carolina. That was when she looked down and saw his trousers, Confederate gray. It was then that she realized that he was a Reb. It didn't matter though, not a lick. He was lying next to a Yank who also could have cared less. The Reb took his remaining hand and reached into his pocket for a letter. Pulling it out he asked if she'd be so kind as to post it for him. He knew he wasn't going to make it. He had written it to his mother a while ago. Jennie had tucked it into her apron pocket and told him not to worry; she'd take care of it. She walked over and set it on the mantle over the fireplace and said, "Let's not forget to get this posted as soon as we're able."

Dewdrops were glistening in her hair and her dress was damp from the mist outside. I remember she looked down at her apron and was upset to see spots of blood smeared across the front of the fresh whiteness. Reaching into her pocket her fingers closed again around that special little portrait perhaps wondering if Jack Skelly were in this predicament, would someone be there caring for him. She looked down for just one quick comforting peek. You could see the shock in her eyes and hear the gasp when she saw the blood smear on the picture. Snatching up a corner of her apron she rubbed at it to remove the fresh red blot. Most of it came off. I think she was a bit embarrassed, me seeing how upset she was.

"The soldier," she said, trying to change the subject. "I had to hold his head up so's he could drink. He was very badly wounded." Untying her apron she excused herself and went into the kitchen. I could hear her blowing her nose as she tried to get control. It was going to be a long day and there was lots to do.

It was cooler, but it was also July and we knew it wouldn't last. Jennie seemed to be perking up, and you could tell she was trying to bring back her usual good humor; still there was a haunted look in her eyes that she couldn't hide.

The door closed gently as she returned to the scene in the yard. Now and again she'd come back in to ask me something about caring for the worst of the wounded. I'd had nurse training so I knew a bit, but certainly not enough to help with the carnage outside. The best I could do was to tell her to try to keep the wounds covered and make them comfortable until a doctor could get to them. I think there were more wounded out there than anyone could handle. But she did her best going from one to the other, offering water or bread and a comforting word.

The morning sky started to lighten although there was no sun. It was still cloudy, but the fog was turning wispy and floating gently away. It could have been as lovely a setting as there could ever be except for the groans outside. Jennie already had bread in the ovens and the heavenly smell was wafting through the house. Baby Louis slept so peacefully.

Then it started again, that wretched sound of cannons in an almost unending barrage. Worse, the rifle fire was so close that bullets were hitting the sides of the house. They were embedded in the brick, so Harry had informed us as he brought in our morning supply of water. He shouldn't have even been outside, but there was so much to tend to. Jennie was becoming increasingly agitated. She came into the room and without so much as a by your leave, took Louis from my arms and put him at the foot of the bed.

"Mother," she'd ordered, "Come along with me, I need help with the cook fires." She then turned to me and ordered me to the foot of the bed.

Now Jennie sometimes gets this tone to her voice and it's not a nice tone and as far as I can tell it's an "I mean business" tone. I know when not to cross her. I mean I knew my sister better than anyone else ever did, probably a lot better then Jack Skelly knew her. Well I asked no questions, besides she'd moved Louis down there and he was looking a mite lonely. She took my pillow and moved it to the foot of the bed and left the room. No sooner had she closed the door then all hell broke loose. Mother would be horrified to hear me speak so, but the world exploded. For who knows what reason, those Rebs shot out every last one of our windows. The sound of exploding glass was quite enough to scare us into speechlessness. Glass flew through the air. I did the best I could tucking baby Louis under me. However, no sooner had they shot out all those windows then there was one last shot fired.

That bullet, that last shot, went clean through the bedpost at the foot of my bed, right over my head. It then hit the head of the bed, exactly mind you, I mean exactly where I had just been. Imagine!

Well then the screaming started, worse than ever before. It frightened me so. It was me screaming and I couldn't quit; baby Louis joined in. Mother came back, white as a church spire, very nearly swooning, she was so frightened. Then the two boys who had been hiding under the bed started in.

Jennie, you could see it in her eyes, was willing herself to be brave and not to faint, she was going to handle whatever it was. I know she thought she was going to find both of us mortally wounded. She walked over, almost wooden like, in complete control and stared down at us. There was no blood, but the spent bullet, hot and still smoking, was lying on the mattress at the head of the bed. It had scorched a right fine hole through our best linen sheet.

Soldiers came crashing through the door, so terrorizing us that our screams stopped in our throats. We were sure this was the end. I kept Lewis hidden under the blankets, convinced they were out to do him harm. Jennie drew herself up to her full height and spoke directly to the roomful of wide-eyed soldiers and all she could say was, "If there is anyone in this house that is to be killed today, I hope it is me, as Georgie has that little baby."

The soldiers were all surrounding the bed looking down at me. When they realized there was no blood and I was perfectly fine, they were embarrassed to be in a lady's bed chamber and made a hasty departure, tipping their hats and saying, "Begging your pardon ma'am just wanted to check on you."

They all backed out the door and left Jennie and me and Mother in our now speechless state. The boys flatly refused to come out from under the bed, no matter what Jennie said. She gave me a hug and said that was probably an end to their shooting at the house, there wasn't much more damage they could do. She told the boys they were fine. Actually they were probably less trouble right where they were, so Jennie passed them each a biscuit and a cup of water and told them under the bed was a fine place for a picnic.

You could see her square her shoulders as she walked out of the room. "I've got to get more bread made," she said as she went through the door, and said she'd leave it ajar so she could hear us if we needed anything.

She spoke to us now and again through the open door, asking after our welfare and whether or not we needed anything. We could hear her as she slapped and punched and kneaded the bread, forming loaves and biscuits from the meager supplies we had left. She never stopped. Wonder what she was thinking?

I guess it was near 8:30, the sun had burned off most of the morning fog and the heat had just started rolling through all the shattered windows. We really should have left long ago, which we knew now. It had been foolish to stay, but we didn't know it would come to this and now we had no choice. The gunshots were ringing out all around us. The noise was almost becoming deafening and the smell of fired gunpowder floated through the gaping openings where the windows were supposed to be.

Noise or not, I was getting sleepy just lying there in that bed. I kept Louis snuggled down next to me and the boys were still hiding under the bed. I was trying to decide if I should join them.

An odd sounding shot rang out. Like a thunk almost. It was a different sound. A muffled sound followed, coming from the kitchen. A body falling? I could smell scorched wood, the same smell that was there when the bullet tore through that bedstead just a little bit ago.

I try to remember the rest of it, but it's hazy and a lot of it just doesn't come to me anymore. Mother was at the door, tears in her eyes. No screaming this time. Then the room again filled with soldiers. Jennie was on the floor, her hand outlined in her apron pocket, clutching something. A huge blood spot spreading on the wood kitchen floor.

I remember being led barefoot to the stairs. Then the soldiers. Then saying I would not go without my sister. Then all of us were led up the wood stairs to the second floor. Soldiers banged out the wall where the missile went through just yesterday. The hole was now big enough for people to walk through. Then we were led down the stairs in Miz McClain's side of the house. Then out the door.

More shots fired. I didn't care anymore if they shot me. Just don't shoot my baby, I thought. Then we were led down the stairs into the cellar. Someone had brought my rocker. Gentle hands pushed me down into it. Then I looked up as two soldiers carried in my quilt, the one I'd made when I was just five years old. Jennie always said it was her favorite. My sister was wrapped in that quilt. There was a blot of blood that'd soaked through. I could just make out the little pink hearts that I'd embroidered so long ago with the dark red stain spreading over them.

I watched in a daze. Can't tell you why, there were no tears. Watched as they carried that bundle over to the wood rack, the one where we used to store milk pails. They laid her gently, tenderly down on that rack. Saw one of the soldiers stoop down and pick up something that'd fallen from her pocket. He placed it in her hand and closed her fingers around it. I remember that quite clearly. I saw her hand, the bread dough still clinging to it. It just stuck there. There was a dusting of flour on the sleeve of her light blue dress, the one that she'd changed into just a few hours before.

Louis started fussing. Mother came over to me, put her hand on my shoulder and said I needed to feed my baby. I'm sure I did, but I just can't remember. I know he quieted down. The boys were there. Don't know how they got them down, Isaac being lame and all and Harry, the little wanderer, terrified out of his wits. But I know they were there. I heard a whimper every now and again from one of them, but I couldn't help them. Mother found an old egg box and put it under my feet, then pulled a light shawl over my legs. It was cool in that cellar, cooler then it'd been upstairs in weeks. I can remember that part of it. Don't know much else that went on.

Rocking back and forth, I thought about Jennie. She was my only sister. Had three brothers but only one sister. How could this have happened now? She was my best friend. We loved doing things together when we were little. We shared our clothes, heck we even had to share our bed. We would cover for each other when we were caught doing something wrong. I remember covering for her a lot more then she had to cover for me, but heck, I was supposed to watch out for her. She was younger. Why hadn't I been watching out for her now? How could this happen? How could it happen to my Jennie? She was so good. She was so kind. Everyone loved her. How could this happen to her? I think I dozed off, my mind too numb to grasp what had happened.

The soldiers came down into the cellar. They came to bring Mother back up to finish baking bread. To this day she says she has no idea how she did it; in fact she rarely if ever talks about it. She just knows she did what she was told and for whatever reason recalls making 15 loaves for the soldiers. She just kept going until there was not one trace of flour left in our larder. Nothing was left in the entire house save for a few beans. She said she was going to have a time pulling together a dinner to feed all of us. Night was coming on. One of the soldiers came down with water for all of us and he handed me a quilt. Said it might get cooler with the rain and all and I might need it. I spread it out; it was made up in all shades of red, with deep blues and stark whites. Asked him where he'd gotten it, I'd never seen it before. He just sort of shrugged and said he found it upstairs. I thought maybe it'd come from Miz McClain's side of the house.

Isaac piped up and in that soft way of his said: "It's your birthday present." I had no idea what he meant. Who was it from? "Jennie did it," he said. His words were garbled and he hiccupped once but went on that she'd been working on it for weeks. She had wanted to surprise me. Tomorrow, the 4th of July would be my 22nd birthday. I remember the lump in my throat that I thought was going to strangle me as I looked down and saw the patchwork of our lives. In disbelief I ran my hand over the beautifully worked design.

There were a hundred stories stitched together for all time. Stories from the pieces of fabric cut from our past. There were pieces of worn-thin school dresses. There was one that I remember so well, once a deep sky blue. We'd both worn that dress. It had been taken up and let down and taken in and let back out. It had been our favorite dress; there was even a piece of the sash that had the tiny embroidered flowers on it.

There were memories everywhere that she had carefully sewn together. I recognized a piece of Father's shirt and even pieces of Louis' red bandana. I was stunned but I had to smile at that. I remember that we'd looked high and low for that bandana; he wanted to take it with him when he went off to war and we couldn't find it anywhere. Well of course, Jennie had it, sewing it into the quilt.

There was a piece from the dress that Mother had been sewing for little baby Martha before she died. I remember she was trying to finish that dress before the snow flew and then it was never finished; Martha had died. And then there was a piece from John James' shirt that I was sure must have been part of his uniform. She must have stitched that up one night after we'd all gone to bed. And then a deep blue square from Samuel's first long pants. It seemed so long ago. How had she ever done it without my even knowing?

The quilt was near perfect. A collection of the fabric of our lives, all neatly stitched together. It only needed a border to surround it and enclose all the different pieces.

The candle next to me was sputtering and threatening to burn itself out, but I pulled it closer so's I could make out the small block letters. They were her initials, M.V.W., Mary Virginia Wade, with a date, July 4, 1863. It was enclosed in a thin circle of blue embroidered flowers, forget me nots.

It was so beautiful; I knew it would keep me warm and safe even on the coldest of days. The riot of color and different shapes all pulled together made an intricate and beautiful pattern. It made me think that maybe this is what the Lord did, sending us pieces of life, and then with His help we patched them altogether, to try to make some sense of it.

~ CHAPTER SEVEN ~

Guess I didn't really pull myself together 'til the next day. I had spent the night holding my new quilt and my baby. Imagine if you will, we spent all that time with my sister. I could not bear to look over in that direction. I knew she was there, I could feel it. I didn't need to turn and look.

The boys slept on and off, cried and ate little through that long night. The soldiers had brought down some bread that we all shared. It felt like it turned to sawdust in my mouth. I wasn't sure if I was going to be able to even swallow it. I've just got to say it was the longest, dreariest, night of my life. I know the only reason I got through it was because of baby Louis. He needed me more than I needed to succumb to the misery.

Why? I must've asked that a hundred or a thousand times during the night. She'd just turned 20 years old. I had to try to keep myself together and stop questioning the whys and wherefores. It was now going to fall on my shoulders to hold things together.

It was hard to keep from going over to hold her hand. I know that wooden bench was as cold as it was hard. I wanted to lay her out somewheres else, but where? I wanted to pick her up and hold her in my lap and comfort her and tell her everything would be all right. I wanted to slap her cheeks and tell her to stop it, get up and get on with it. I was mad with her for leaving me like this. I needed her. She was our strength, didn't she know that? How could she be so selfish to leave us? How would I continue on without her?

The boys were quiet, huddled in a corner. They were so upset, especially Isaac. Not sure if he quite understood death but I saw him sitting in a corner staring at the shape wrapped in that precious old quilt. It seemed like he sat there for hours, trying to figure it out. Actually, looking back on it, I think he was trying to will her back to life.

I'm sure he thought that at any moment she was going to rise up and say something like, "Here Isaac, is it time to go out?" Like Isaac, guess I was kind of hoping it wasn't true. She wasn't really gone. Truth be known, as the soldiers were carrying her down, I heard them talking among themselves. They said it was a random shot, could've been fired from either side. Didn't really matter, I guess. It had passed right through her and pierced her heart and there was no taking it back.

The night went on forever. I can still feel that hard rocker that I sat in through the night. After sunset there were still random shots, enough to keep Harry in the cellar and not running about getting in everyone's way. When one of the soldiers brought bread and some drinking water down, he said, "Ma'am it's about over, but I'd stay put a spell. Still a few shots being fired."

He was so kind. He touched my shoulder and could barely get the words out, "I'm sorry for your troubles ma'am." He looked as though he was about to cry. Thought about getting up to try to comfort him, but he was gone before I could readjust baby Louis and get to my feet. The soldiers had brought down that old rocker that'd been in the family probably since Adam met Eve. Not any too comfortable, but better than lying on the dirt floor. I was probably a deal more comfortable then the two boys sitting in the corner on Isaac's quilt. There was a candle too that one of the soldiers brought down, it cast a bit of light. Seemed a mite eerie actually.

Guess I've got to own up to it. I was a bit edgy the entire night. I mean with Jennie lying there and all, I was pretty glad to have the two boys with me and the baby. Young as they were, they were still some sort of company.

I spent some time musing over how to get word to Jack Skelly. 'Course we didn't know at the time about him. Didn't find that out until a few days later. Anyway I had baby Louis to comfort and love too so that pretty much got me through the night. That and snuggling with my quilt remembering and touching each piece.

Many hours later when it felt like morning, I crept over to the cellar door, wondering what a new day would bring. It was dismal. I was not surprised. The dawn was coming on cloudy and rainy and overcast and miserable. It certainly fit our moods. I crept back to the rocker, determined to keep the boys spirits up, but really wasn't all that successful.

Ended up spending most of the morning watching a pretty little moth flit around, back and forth - back and forth near the flame of the sputtering candle. Flirting with danger it was. Wanted to tell that pretty little creature not to get too close to the flame or she'd get her wings burned. Waved the little thing away and she danced about flitting around maybe looking for a safe place to land. I watched as the bright little creature bounced around up near the wood rafters, splintery with age. Spider haven it was up there. Not watching where she was going or perhaps not knowing the danger she flitted right into one of the many spider webs. She was caught. I had watched that lively little moth for close to an hour and didn't want to see it tangled up like that so pulled down the web and ever so carefully freed that tiny winged creature. I watched as she flew off. I sat back down and continued my vigil.

We stayed in that cellar until 1 o'clock in the afternoon. The boys must have been getting antsy, as they had nothing with them except the one lead soldier that Isaac had tucked in his pocket. They played war games trying to dig in the dirt floor and make hills and valleys and such, but with just one soldier to play with it wasn't that much fun. They tried to ignore the body wrapped in the quilt, but it was a small room and she was right there.

When the soldiers remembered us in the early afternoon, two of them came down to the cellar. One I'd seen before, maybe he was the one that helped us get out of the house, couldn't quite place him, just knew his face. The other was a complete stranger, older with a heavy New England accent. Very nice, both of them. They offered to carry me, "Ma'am if you'll allow, we'd be pleased to lift you up those stairs and around to your house."

Told them, no, I'd be fine. Truth was I was feeling a bit woozy again, but I was determined I was going to make it on my own. There was going to be lots to do and I was tired of being an invalid.

The older one with the New England accent talked a lot like Mr. Goodwin, our grocer who had lived up in Boston before he moved down our way. Anyway that older soldier saw Isaac and his lame condition and he just scooped him up easy as you please and said something like, "Well young man at least I can help you."

They took us up the cellar stairs and round the house, through the drizzle and mud. They walked real slow, I took the arm of the younger one, he kind of steadied me. He said not to worry about Jennie, they'd take care of it for us. Asked if it'd be OK to bury her in the backyard. "'Course," I said, "We'd like to keep her close by."

Well I may as well mention what we saw on that short walk. I mean maybe that's why I wasn't so steady on my feet. It was not the same town it was just a few days ago. In fact, if I didn't know it to be true, I'd have thought we were in some horrible bad dream.

What came to mind was "the storm." Six or seven years ago we had a most terrible blow. It was a windstorm like no other I'd ever seen. It was probably in September, early September as I recollect. Well that storm was so bad, we had trees uprooted and the ones left were shredded of their leaves. Shingles were ripped off most of the houses. Picture that only times ten. That's what was waiting for us.

The town was destroyed. There were dead and dying wherever you looked. Soldiers everywhere. There were carts trying to make their way up the street carrying all manner of wounded and those past helping. There were mule and horse carcasses, and I even saw Miz Bayley's cow, dead, shot through and through. But it was the sounds that were most bothersome. The moans and crying of the wounded. It wasn't just outside the window anymore, it was everywhere.

It seemed there were holes shot in every square inch of the houses. All the windows for as far as I could see had been shot out. Add to this an already drizzly gray, hot and humid afternoon. This must, I thought, be what Hell is like. It was the longest walk I've ever taken.

Every yard that I could see was trampled into nothingness. Every fence had been knocked over. The soldier whose arm I was holding, actually clinging to at this point, tried to protect me and hide it from me, but there was no possible way to hide what had happened here. It was everywhere for as far as I could see. Bodies, debris, dead animals, overturned carts, men limping using fence posts for crutches, front doors lying in the street. I could see women, most of them I knew, crying in their handkerchiefs. There was a dog, crying pitifully, limping his way up the street, dragging behind him his crippled leg.

The soldiers. It was nearly indescribable. They all looked as though they were the walking dead, their faces blank and their eyes staring at nothing. They all had some wound or other. Every one of them was bloodied. What indescribable carnage must've taken place. At one point, I thought I was going to collapse. That kind soldier pretty much carried me the last few feet to our kitchen.

That was where I had to face the next shock. He tried to turn me so's I wouldn't see the hole in the kitchen door. I saw it all right and then I tried not to look, but there was a very large reddish brown stain on the kitchen floor. It couldn't be helped. I gave in and just let the soldier pick me up and carry me to my bed. I clung to Louis, fearing I'd faint and drop him. My front room, the one that my bed was in was an impossible mess. Broken glass, the bed in complete disarray, the bullet hole in my bedpost, a reminder of what almost happened. It was more then I could take in all at once. I closed my eyes and thankfully fell sound asleep.

"Georgie," said Mother, "C'mon along. You need to get up." She was shaking my shoulder and none too easy. She'd said something about Jennie, but my mind couldn't make sense of it.

"What about Jennie?" I asked, rubbing sleep from my eyes. She looked down at me, and as tears came to her eyes, I remembered. She brought me a glass of water and wet rag and started mopping at my face.

"Well?"

"It's time," she said.

"Time?" I asked, looking at the clock. But the clock had obviously stopped. The pendulum was silent. There was no ticking. The room was quiet. The clock had stopped at 8:30. Curious I thought. That's when it happened, but Mother was pulling at me.

Don't know quite how it all got through to me exactly, what she was talking about. She took Louis and put him down in his cradle and she told me to shake out my dress somewhat and rewind my hair and try to look presentable.

We walked out the door. The kitchen door, the one with the bullet hole and walked 'round back. It was raining again. The mud was thick and squishy and with each step more stuck to our shoes. It made sucking sounds as we lifted each foot, making each step more difficult.

Samuel was there. Mother must've sent word

that it was OK for him to come out of hiding. The Rebs were gone. They had more important things on their mind than keeping tabs on one civilian boy who they mistook for a horse thief.

Harry was there, staring down into that gaping hole. He was actually tossing pebbles in, watching them splash, creating small ripples across the muddy water. Grandma was there too. Don't know how Mother got this altogether. Not like her at all to take charge. Anyhow, you could tell Grams was having a terrible time. It was probably true, Jennie had been her favorite.

Anyway, that hole, that dark muddy hole in the ground was rapidly filling with rain or maybe it was Gram's tears. Whatever, there were at least three or four inches of water at the bottom. Not a terribly deep hole I might mention, and some of the sides were already starting to collapse in they were so swollen with rain.

Those soldiers certainly had put themselves out to dig it. I mean three or four days of intense battle, going through all the horror that war had to offer, and then they were still able to marshal enough strength to dig a grave for one lone civilian girl.

We were so thankful. Have no idea on this

earth what we would've done without their help. Somehow they'd managed to find a coffin. A very plain walnut box, but well made. They had it just around the side of the house and I couldn't see it, but I could plainly hear them as they pounded each of those nails in to close the lid.

Later I heard that the coffin was meant for a Confederate officer, but guess they left town too fast to worry about it. Anyway we all did the best we could. There were a few soldiers there and just our very small family, not even a preacher to say a few words. I regretted that, there wasn't much we could do about it though.

It was a matter of mere minutes before they lowered that coffin. It was still pouring down rain and gray and as dismal as our Pennsylvania weather can get. When they lowered that coffin I heard a splash as it hit bottom, which sent a shiver up my spine. Think maybe Grams heard it too. She started to teeter a bit, I mean at her age and all, it was some surprise that she was still able to stand. She probably shouldn't have been out in all that rain. But as she teetered, two soldiers appeared instantly at her sides and held her up.

We turned and walked back into the house after that older soldier, the one from New England, had thrown in the first shovel of dirt. That sound will never leave me. It was a solid wet thunk that slammed into my heart. I came back in, absolutely soaked through, and was looking for anything dry to put on when I heard this very quiet weeping, but there was no one there. Kind of sent goose bumps up and down my arms. Then I heard a little boy snort type of noise and realized it was coming from under the bed. I bent down and pulled back the spread and there was Isaac, sobbing his eyes out. Tried to coax him out, but he wanted no part of it. The coaxing only seemed to make it worse. He was about breaking my heart with those no-time-to-breathe sobs. Bless him. His hair was stuck out in all directions, as always.

I got down on the floor on my hands and knees and crawled under the bed to be with him. Not much room if you'd like to know. But that poor little boy, he was nearly beside himself with grief. I laid down next to him and put my arms around him. I pulled his favorite quilt up around his little shoulders and then the two of us rocked back and forth, under the bed, clinging to each other, waiting for our sobs to subside.

~ CHAPTER EIGHT ~

Had to reach Jack Skelly. He needed to know. But the dead, the dying and the wounded, they cried out for care. The tragedy that was unfolding just outside our door. Writing to Jack Skelly was just going to have to wait. His momma had probably already heard. Still wanted to write to him though, so's he'd hear it from me.

Our town, Gettysburg, was nearly destroyed. Looking back on it now I wonder how on this earth did we all pull together to get things back to rights. It took a powerful long time to get it all up and running again. And it was going to be a much longer time I can tell you before people could or would ever forget.

Seems like it was just a few days after the awful business was over with, or the shooting anyway, that everything began to stink so bad we started to wear handkerchiefs over our noses. It was hard to find all the bodies but you knew they were out there.

I'd had some nurse training so I went about trying to be helpful. Some 14,000 of ours were wounded and needing attention, 19,000 of theirs. Can you imagine the like? How do you even count numbers like that? About 7,000 were dead. There were only 2,400 people who lived in our town and many of them were off fighting the war. By my calculation that's about ten wounded for every living, breathing, walking mortal in the town.

Thankfully the Rebs carried off most of their own, but there were some left. They weren't the first that we tended to, but I'll say this, we didn't ignore them either. We tried to get to all of them. But there always seemed to be more.

Mother took over with Louis as best she could and I tried to help out some at the field hospitals. Doc Brown wasn't any too pleased to see me when he found himself working next to me. We were both bending over a litter carrying a very young soldier, who didn't look any older then Samuel. He had a gut wound as they called it. He wasn't going to make it, we knew that, but we worked at making him comfortable. Anyhow, Doc looked up and saw it was me, said I should be home in bed. But then he just shook his head and walked off. He looked like one of the walking wounded. He probably hadn't slept in days.

So much misery. Hard to describe what we saw there. So many injured and we had so few supplies to aid them with. There were gunshot wounds and shrapnel wounds on every conceivable part of a man. Parts of their bodies were just plain missing: an eye, an arm, part of a foot or a whole leg. There were lines that had been permanently worn into faces, mostly from the pain, but also from the fear of their fate, I was quite sure. How were they going to go home and work their farms or their trades, with lost limbs? There were men there that had been blacksmiths, printers, haberdashers, dairy farmers and storekeepers. There was a carriage maker and a sailor. What would they tell their families? As for the others, gangrene sets in fast. The doctors tried to keep up with it, but it was near impossible. They did what they could with what they had.

The heat and lack of food was sapping all of our energy, but we all worked on. People gave whatever they had left. The women of the town came in to try to help; they could wash bandages, redress wounds, write letters, or help to feed the wounded. It was never enough though; we couldn't seem to get ahead of it. It was so distressing. So many were lost and many of them were so young.

During those first few days the men who were left in town, old men and young boys mostly - well they just kept bringing in more wounded on their makeshift litters. The bodies were everywhere: in buildings, wedged down between the rocks on Cemetery Hill, scattered in cornfields and up in the attics of private homes where they'd been stationed as sharpshooters. They found them in the most unlikely places: under carts, behind houses, in cellars or lying there with dead horses fallen on top of them.

Then the dead. They weren't being tended to quickly enough. There was not a more gruesome task. The bodies had started to bloat in the hot July sun and had to be collected soon. Just the stench was going to drive everyone from town.

What struck me most during the first few days was the eerie quiet. A quiet occasionally punctured by the cries from the wounded. It was frightening. People weren't talking. If they had anything to say, it was in whispers. Birds weren't singing, there was no low throaty mooing from the cows, or whinnying from the horses and no chatter from the children running through the streets. There weren't even dogs barking. The breeze couldn't rustle the leaves in the trees, cause there were no leaves. The world had changed. Even wild little Harry must have realized the solemnity of the occasion; he slinked around in the shadows, offering to help where he could.

So Jack Skelly. What was I to do about Jennie's intended? Maybe what happened was good, maybe not. Who's to know? Anyways I never did write that letter. Turned out Miz Skelly and I were both working in the hospital tents that had been set up just outside of town. It was later in the month. Mother was still tending to baby Louis for me. But there she was, Miz Skelly, standing right in front of me. She looked the devil, I have to say that. I should've known the minute I saw her, but instead she took me in her arms and patted me on the back and told me how very sorry she was about Jennie. Was there anything she could do?

She wasn't very tall, in fact a bit stout, so when she hugged me her head came up to about my bosom. I'd lost so much weight that her arms easily slid around me. I opened my mouth to ask for Jack's address so that I could write to him, but before I could say a word she took me by the hand to a bench just outside the tent. The sun was making its slow descent in preparation for the night, but the heat from the day was still radiating up from the hard–packed, trampled earth.

As we sat together and watched the glory of the late evening sunset, with all its pinks and yellows and oranges radiating out from it, she said something about the beauty of the setting sun and how there'll always be another day.

She hesitated a moment and then in a hushed voice told me that Jack had been wounded at Carter's Woods in Winchester, Virginia, back sometime in June. The letter she received just a few days ago said it was on the 15th. We knew nothing about this. Within a few short weeks, on July 12th, she said, Jack Skelly died of that wound. She was somehow able to tell me this while holding back the sorrow.

We're quite sure Jennie didn't know of this but who's to say for sure? Maybe she felt something and just didn't want to talk about it. We sat there together watching the sun slip below the horizon. There were more unshed tears to come. But for now we would get some comfort from knowing they're together forever. And even though fate kept them apart in this world they will never again be apart.

We stood and walked, arm in arm, in no great rush, 'til nearly dark, then together returned to our places to try to erase more of what remained of the horror that had taken place.

Later, after much of the scars of battle had been removed, we learned that Jennie had been the only civilian killed in that horrific battle. But, we knew we were just two of the many who had lost so much. No one would ever forget what had happened here, but together we would forge on to somehow meet and accept the challenges as each new day unfolded.

~ EPILOGUE ~

The clock did stop at 8:30 that fateful day in 1863. It hangs in the parlor in the Jenny Wade House in Gettysburg. Not long after the end of the Civil War, Mary Virginia (Jennie) Wade was moved from her shallow grave in the backyard of the Baltimore Street home to a new resting place near the German Reformed Church. In November 1865, Louis McClellan, Georgie's husband and John James, Jennie's brother, moved her remains to the family plot in the Evergreen Cemetery. The plot, marked by a monument is only a few hundred feet away from the grave site of Johnston Hastings Skelly, Jr., otherwise known as Jack.

BIBLIOGRAPHY

Chang, Ina. A SEPARATE BATTLE. New York: Puffin Books, 1991.

Coco, Gregory A. WAR STORIES. Gettysburg, Thomas Publications, 1992.

Garrison, Webb THE UNKNOWN CIVIL WAR. Nashville: Cumberland House Publishing, Inc., 2000.

Grimm, Herbert L., Roy, Paul L. and Rose, George. HUMAN INTEREST STORIES OF THE THREE DAYS' BATTLES AT GETTYSBURG. Gettysburg: Gem Inc., 1995.

Hawthorne, Frederick W., GETTYSBURG: STORIES OF MEN AND MONUMENTS. Gettysburg: The Association of Licensed Battlefield Guides, 1988.

Johnston, J.W. THE TRUE STORY OF "JENNIE" WADE. Rochester: J.W. Johnston, 1917.

Leisch, Juanita. CIVIL WAR CIVILIANS. Gettysburg, Thomas Publications, 1994.

Moore, John Hammond. THE CONFEDERATE HOUSEWIFE. Columbia: Summerhouse Press, 1997.

Riley, Mara. WHATEVER SHALL I WEAR? Graphic Fine Arts Press, 2002.

Seymour, John. THE FORGOTTEN ARTS & CRAFTS. New York: Dorling Kindersley, 2001.

Storrick, W.C. GETTYSBURG. New York: Barnes and Noble, 1994.

Ward, Geoffrey C. with Ric and Ken Burns, THE CIVIL WAR. New York: Alfred A. Knopf, Inc., 1990

ANTIETAM - WAKING THE FURY

Emily at 15 is bored and annoyed with just about everything and everybody. Tired of her chores and irritated by the endless care of three younger sisters, she would like to have a life of her own. Her parents are absent; her Father is off fighting a war she doesn't understand and her Mother has left for Pennsylvania. As the eldest of the four sisters, she must take responsibility for her home and family. When the bloodiest battle of the Civil War is fought almost on her doorstep she is unwillingly pressed into service. Emily is called on to make decisions and to take charge of wounded soldiers while fending off the invading troops and protecting her younger sisters. Life changes forever as she discovers a courage that she did not know she possessed. Strengths emerge as she stands up for her beliefs while sheltering the enemy and caring for a runaway slave, both of which hold very serious consequences. In this remarkably accurate depiction of the Battle of Antietam, a legend is once more uncovered. It involves a mass of very angry bees. This dangerous, stinging swarm may well have had an influence on the outcome of that fateful day in 1862.

Now available at Amazon, Nook, Kobo and other online retailers in print and digital editions!

THE LETTER

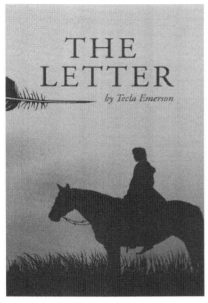

"My being forever banished from your sight..."

Just who was this "...undutiful and Disobedient Child" who in 1756 penned a letter to her father in England?

What had she done to so offend him?

Why, as an extremely well-educated young girl, had she become an indentured servant? Why was she alone? In her letter, she pleads with her father to forgive her and to at least send her a bit of clothing. "...almost naked, no shoes nor stockings to wear."

Here, within these pages, the mystery of Elizabeth Sprigs is revealed. It is a tale based on a single letter sent from Baltimore so long ago.

Now available at Amazon, Nook, Kobo and other online retailers in print and digital editions!

Made in the USA
Middletown, DE
06 July 2023